WALKS IN THE WILDS
OF CAMBRIDGESHIRE

WALKS
IN THE WILDS
OF CAMBRIDGESHIRE

Fowlmere Nature Reserve

Josie Briggs
With illustrations by the author

JOHN NICKALLS PUBLICATIONS

Dedication

For Elsie

First published 2004

© Josie C Briggs 2004

ISBN 1 904136 18 4

Published by John Nickalls Publications
Oak Farm Bungalow, Sawyers Lane, Suton
Wymondham, Norfolk NR18 9SH

Designed by Ashley Gray and Printed by Geo R Reeve Ltd,
9–11 Town Green, Wymondham, Norfolk, NR18 0BD

CONTENTS

Front cover: Chippenham Fen.

Back cover: Hills and Holes, Barnack.

INTRODUCTION

ANYONE who tells you that Norfolk is flat obviously has not been to Cambridgeshire. Much of the county was once low-lying fen, until it was drained over the centuries to produce rich farmland. Draining the peaty soil caused the land to shrink; now much of it is around, or even below, sea level.

Maps of parts of Cambridgeshire resemble a geometry diagram. The land is criss-crossed by straight roads, drainage dykes and re-routed rivers. In places the rivers are higher than the surrounding farmland, and hemmed in by embankments. Drainage must be continuous, by means of pumping stations where necessary.

Paxton Pits.

The friendly cows on Upwood Meadows.

In the past, settlements were built on the higher parts: natural or man-made 'islands', linked by causeways. Some of these developed into town and cities, which stand out clearly from many miles away across the plain.

Most of Cambridgeshire's nature reserves and conservation sites are small and scattered, remnants of ancient fen and woodland (sometimes both in one site). They really are oases for wildlife.

Staff and volunteers of various organisations work hard to maintain the sites, which provide important wetland, grassland and woodland habitats. Conservation bodies include Bedfordshire, Cambridgeshire and Northamptonshire Wildlife Trust; English Nature; the RSPB; Cambridge Protection Society, and various local councils and landowners. All are doing an excellent job, for which walkers and nature lovers can be grateful.

Josie Briggs

ACKNOWLEDGEMENTS

I would like to thank the following for their help and information on the nature reserves and conservation sites: English Nature (Hills and Holes, Chippenham Fen); Bedfordshire, Cambridgeshire and Northamptonshire Wildlife Trust (Brampton Wood, Upwood Meadows, Ouse Washes, Roswell Pits, Waresley and Gransden Woods); RSPB (Ouse Washes, Fowlmere); Huntingdonshire District Council's Countryside Services (Paxton Pits); Cambridge Protection Society (Wandlebury Ring).

I am particularly grateful to my husband, Andrew, for planning the routes, accompanying me on all the walks, and checking the manuscript.

ABOUT THE AUTHOR

Josie Briggs lives in Norfolk with her husband Andrew and her cat Shannon, and enjoys exploring East Anglia's countryside with its wildlife habitats. She is interested in conservation and organic gardening and has contributed articles to several magazines, including *Organic Gardening, Suffolk and Norfolk Life, Country Gardens and Smallholdings, Amateur Gardening, The Countryman* and *Aquarist and Pondkeeper*. Her first book, *Walks in the Wilds of Norfolk* (S. B. Publications, 1998), was followed by *Walks in the Wilds of Suffolk* (S. B. Publications, 2001) and *Curiosities of Norfolk* (John Nickalls Publications, 2002). She has also written a book about wildlife gardening, *Creating Small Habitats for Wildlife in your Garden* (Guild of Master Craftsman Publications, 2000, 2002, 2003).

Josie is also a tutor in science and mathematics, and gives lectures on wildlife gardening and related topics.

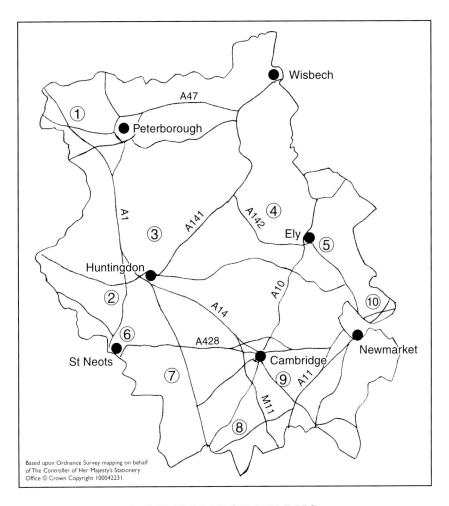

Based upon Ordnance Survey mapping on behalf
of The Controller of Her Majesty's Stationery
Office © Crown Copyright 100042231.

LOCATION OF WALKS

1 Hills and Holes, Barnack

2 Brampton Wood Nature Reserve

3 Upwood Meadows Nature Reserve

4 Ouse Washes Nature Reserve, Manea

5 Roswell Pits, Ely

6 Paxton Pits Nature Reserve

7 Waresley and Gransden Woods

8 Fowlmere Nature Reserve

9 Wandlebury Ring and Beechwoods Nature Reserve

10 Chippenham Fen Nature Reserve

KEY TO MAPS

1 Maps are drawn to scale.

2 Numbers on maps are points of interest referred to in the text.

3 P denotes car parking.

4 Dotted lines denote boundaries of woods.

5 Other symbols as on Ordnance Survey maps.

THE WALKERS' CODE

1 Keep to marked paths and trails.

2 Fasten gates behind you.

3 Keep dogs under control (dogs are not allowed in some nature reserves).

4 Do not drop litter.

5 Do not disturb wildlife or livestock.

6 Do not pick or dig up any plants.

7 On roads without footpaths, keep to the right facing oncoming traffic.

8 Obey any rules specific to a site (see display boards at entrances to reserves).

Walk 1 – HILLS AND HOLES, BARNACK

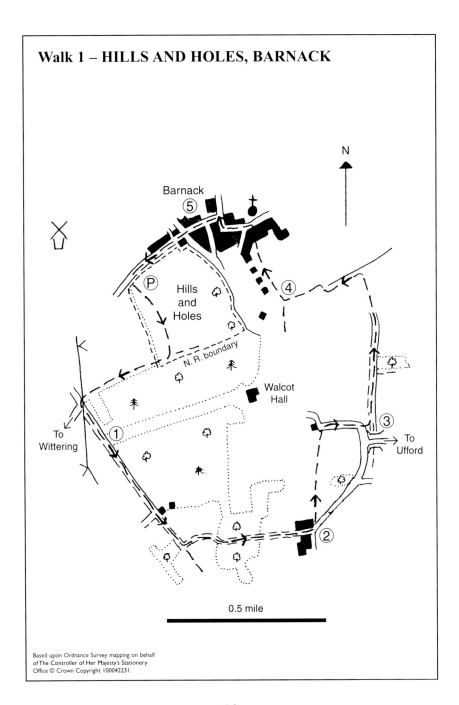

Based upon Ordnance Survey mapping on behalf
of The Controller of Her Majesty's Stationery
Office © Crown Copyright 100042231.

Walk 1

HILLS AND HOLES, BARNACK

Distance: 3.5 miles

Map: OS Landranger 142

Start/Parking: The lay-by at the north-west corner of Hills and Holes Nature Reserve; grid ref. TF 073047. (If this is full, there is a small car park at the reserve's entrance, a short way towards Barnack.)

Nearest town: Peterborough

THE aerial photograph on the front of Barnack Hills and Holes information leaflet (from English Nature) shows clearly why this national nature reserve received its mysterious name. A large field adjacent to Barnack village is rumpled and puckered like a sheet in need of ironing. It is no less curious from the ground: the grassland undulates spectacularly, the result of limestone quarrying centuries ago.

Leaving the nature reserve, this walk continues by skirting much of the boundary of Walcot Hall estate, then crosses farmland and follows a disused railway to Barnack village, with its welcome Millstone public house.

Hills and Holes Nature Reserve can be explored freely, but please keep to the paths.

Route directions

Go through the wooden gate next to the metal one. Follow the track a short way, then pass through the next gate into a paddock. There is an information board here about the nature reserve and its inhabitants.

Entrance to Hills and Holes.

Continue through the kissing gate and follow the track ahead. The 'hills and holes' are evident here, coated with grass and meadow flowers. Moles and rabbits burrow into the light soil, leaving cavities and spoil heaps everywhere.

The path eventually enters a small wood. Turn right at the tall dry-stone wall ahead, and leave the nature reserve through a gate. This wall marks the boundary of Walcot Hall estate, but trees hide the hall. Follow the wall along the left edge of a large agricultural field. Barnack windmill is visible over the field to the right.

The stone wall veers left at a pylon. Leave the field and turn left on to the lane, then go through the gate on to the Hereward Way bridleway. The wall reappears on the left, and there is a good view over fields to the right. After a short distance, Walcot Hall is visible behind a wooden gate (1), at the end of a long avenue.

Continue ahead at the estate corner. The countryside around here consists of gently undulating fields dotted with woods. The Hereward Way continues ahead, but keep on the main track which turns sharp left. The path enters open woodland where lots of new trees have been planted to fill the gaps, and descends gently before emerging from the trees cover.

A gate (2) blocks the way ahead, but pedestrians can go through a

14

gap on the right. The path passes between farm buildings. On reaching the lane, go over the stile on the left and follow the left field boundary towards a large house. Through the next gate, there is a clear path across an arable field. Go right at the road. The road bends right, but descend the bank on the left and take the path along what used to be a railway, walking away from the old bridge (3). There are hedges on both sides, then the path passes a small overgrown copse on the right. You may glimpse Walcot Hall, partly shielded by trees, beyond open fields to the left. Barnack church's stumpy spire is visible ahead left.

The stumpy spire of Barnack church

At the field corner, turn left and follow the stream. At the end of this field, a small clump of trees surrounds a stagnant pool. Go left at the hedge, keeping the hedge to your right, then turn right between two wooden posts at the corner of the cricket ground (4). The narrow path goes between trees, their branches meeting overhead, before emerging between buildings opposite Barnack Church.

Turn left along the road, and left again at Main Street. There is an unusual wooden door in a stone archway (5) on the right, set into a high wall. A plaque on the door reads: 'This thirteenth century arch stood in the parish church as part of the dividing wall between the tower and the nave. It was removed in 1855 and re-erected in the wall of the rectory (now Kingsley House). It was removed to this site in 1963'.

Turning left diverts you to the village inn.

Main Street becomes School Lane. Over the crossroad, the lane climbs gently, leaves the village and returns to the car park at Hills and Holes.

History and wildlife

English Nature owns and manages the 22-hectare Hills and Holes, designat-ed as a National Nature

Barnack's 13th century arch.

Reserve in 1977 to protect its endangered habitats and wildlife.

Quarrying for limestone began at this site 1500 years ago by the Romans, and continued until 1500, when all the useful stone had been extracted. The quality stone, called Barnack rag, was used to construct Peterborough and Ely Cathedrals, and many other famous buildings. Since the quarry closed, a rich variety of grasses and wildflowers gradually colonised the spoil heaps.

There used to be more grassland of this type in the area, but devel-opment of the land has caused most of it to be lost. Hills and Holes contains over half of Cambridgeshire's remaining limestone grass-land.

Some rare wildflowers grow here, including the yellow and purple pasque flower. In spring, cowslips and violets make a colourful show. The best time to see Hills and Holes' wildflowers, though, is June and

July, when nine different types of orchids flower, as well as many other varieties of lime-loving plants.

All these flowers attract butterflies and other insects. Yellow ants' nests are dotted around the site, small mounds of earth that help keep the occupants warm by absorbing the sun's rays.

Many birds, including jays and green woodpeckers, shelter in the reserve's scrub and woodland.

Sheep graze for three months every autumn to keep the grass short and encourage the wildflowers to grow. English Nature staff and volunteers control the scrub and young trees that continually try to take over.

Places of interest

Wansford Station, a few miles south of Hills and Holes, is the starting point for the Nene Valley Steam Railway. A variety of steam engines and rolling stock operate on this seven-mile track. There is also a museum, engine shed and shop.

Ferry Meadows, occupying a six-mile stretch of the Nene Valley west of Peterborough, provides a variety of activities including water sports, horse riding, bird watching and walking round the lakes and meadows.

Another good place for water sports is Tallington Lakes Leisure Park, north of Barnack, one of Britain's largest water sports centres.

Peakirk Waterfowl Gardens, north of Peterborough, is home to more than seven hundred waterfowl in its twenty acres of ponds and gardens.

Peterborough itself has a good variety of shops, restaurants and other facilities. Its twelfth century cathedral is said to have the finest west front in Europe, and there are magnificent thirteenth century paintings on the nave ceiling.

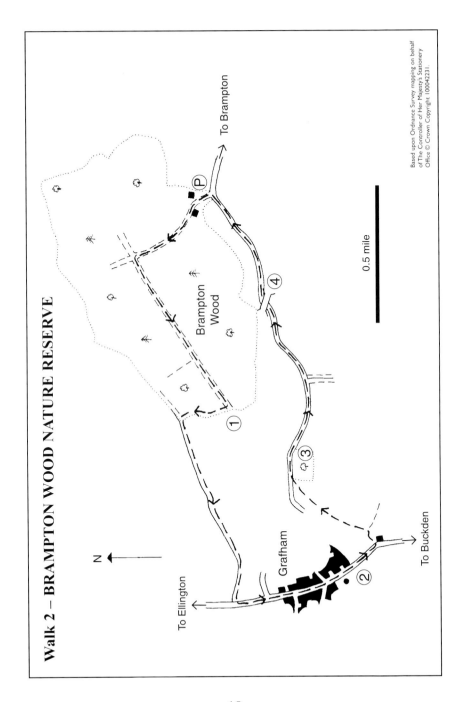

Walk 2 – BRAMPTON WOOD NATURE RESERVE

N

To Brampton

P

Brampton Wood

To Ellington

Grafham

To Buckden

① ② ③ ④

0.5 mile

Walk 2

BRAMPTON WOOD NATURE RESERVE

Distance: 4 miles

Map: OS Landranger 153

Start/Parking: Brampton Wood car park; grid ref. TL 185698

Nearest town: Huntingdon

BRAMPTON Wood is the second largest wood in Cambridgeshire, and is criss-crossed by wide pathways called rides. Made a Site of Special Scientific Interest in 1954, it is an important refuge for a variety of flowers, fungi, butterflies, birds and mammals.

Most of the rest of the walk is among arable fields, with flower-lined ditches, hedgerows and a hidden moat to provide interest. It passes through Grafham, a small village near Grafham Water, which is a large reservoir with water sports, visitor centres and its own nature reserves on the shore.

Paths are mostly good, although a bit overgrown near the edges of Brampton Wood. Dogs may enter the wood if they are kept under control. Please keep to the paths and rides in the nature reserve. This walk has one stile.

Route directions

Take the metal gate into the wood. An information board tells of the history and wildlife of this nature reserve. Follow the ride ahead; this open, sunny ride contrasts with the shade under the trees. Grassland wildflowers line the way in summer, serviced by clouds of butterflies

Entrance to Brampton Wood.

and bees. Soon you come to a shelter with more information boards on its wall. It is worth taking a few minutes to read these and familiarise yourself with what you might spot in the wood.

At the crossroad with another wide ride, turn left. The flowers here are those of damp meadows: sedge, purple loosestrife and willow herb. This long straight ride gradually becomes narrower and more overgrown, with branches meeting overhead on the last stretch. The gate at the end (1) is wired shut. Grafham church spire peeps above the trees beyond the field ahead.

Take the narrow path along the woodland edge to the right, then go through the gap in the wire fence at the wood's north-west corner. Cross the wooden bridge to the left and follow the wide path along the edge of a massive field. The parallel ditch on the right supports lush wetland wildflowers, dominated by great hairy willow herb, its carmine flowers making a pretty display in summer. Soon an old hedgerow, now mostly oak and ash trees, appears by the ditch and follows it as far as the road ahead.

At the road, turn left towards Grafham. This road is part of the Three Shires Way Long Distance Path. Continue through the village. Just past the water tower (2) on the right, you can glimpse Grafham Water in the distance beyond the fields.

Turn left along the public footpath, just before a large house. The path curves right; take the left path at the marker post and cross the field towards a small wood. Enter this wood at the marker post, then cross the stile on to a road. The Ordnance Survey map marks a moat (3) where this wood grows, but it is fenced off and nothing is visible among the trees.

Go right along the quiet lane, which gradually becomes leafier as it passes between hedgerows and small trees. The road passes beneath an old iron railway bridge (4), then follows Brampton Wood boundary back to the car park on the left.

History and wildlife

Owned by the Bedfordshire, Cambridgeshire and Northamptonshire Wildlife Trust, this large wood (132 hectares) has been managed as a nature reserve since 1992. It is an old wood, with oak and ash trees growing here since at least 1086, and hazel coppice. Now Brampton Wood contains a rich variety of native trees and shrubs, either colonised or planted: these include blackthorn, hawthorn, field maple, crab apple, wild pear, spindle, birch, aspen and sallow. There are also groups of recently planted conifers. Fragrant-flowered honeysuckle scrambles up some trees. Brampton Wood now supports over three hundred plant species, as well as butterflies, birds and small mammals. Muntjac and fallow deer roam the woods, and dormice were introduced in 1992. Log piles and dead trees support an interesting variety of fungi.

The rides, used for timber transport, are mown in late summer. This regime encourages a mixture of grassland wildflowers to flourish.

21

Information shelter, Brampton Wood.

Places of interest

Grafham Water, a large Anglian Water reservoir, is worth a visit while you are in the area. There is an exhibition centre, a visitor centre, restaurants, picnic sites, water sports and nature trails. If you still have some energy left after your walk, you could hire a bike and explore the cycle lanes around the water. There is a charge for car parking.

Hinchingbrooke Country Park, between Brampton and Huntingdon, also has water sports, but on a smaller scale than at Grafham Water. Or you could take a stroll through its woods and around its lakes. Nearby Hinchingbrooke House was a thirteenth century Benedictine nunnery, and once the home of the Earls of Sandwich. It is set in sixty acres of parkland.

Oliver Cromwell, lord protector of England (1653–58), was born in Huntingdon in 1599 and educated at the town's grammar school. The Cromwell Museum, Huntingdon, displays documents and portraits of Cromwell as well as more contemporary exhibits.

Old iron railway bridge.

Walk 3 – UPWOOD MEADOWS NATURE RESERVE

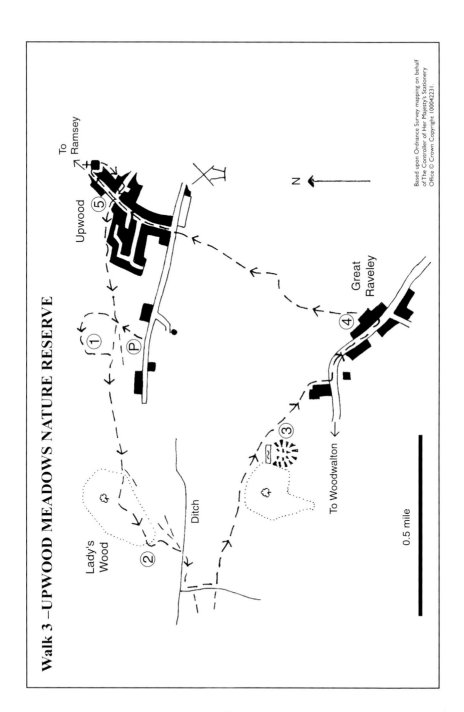

24

Walk 3

UPWOOD MEADOWS NATURE RESERVE

Distance: 3.5 mile

Map: OS Landranger 142

Start/Parking: Upwood Meadows car park, near the end of a dirt track leading west out of Upward; grid ref. TL 252824

Nearest town: Ramsey

UPWOOD Meadows National Nature Reserve is unique among all the other Cambridgeshire conservation sites that we visited. The other nature reserves of this county are mainly fen or woodland or both. Upwood Meadows, on the other hand, consists simply of three fields with cows in them.

What makes these meadows different from the surrounding ones is that they are a rare remnant of Midland clay grassland. Part of the site has never been treated with herbicides or fertilisers, and as a result supports a rich flora of ancient grassland.

The walk first explores this important reserve, then crosses fields to the diminutive Lady's Wood, an ancient coppice consisting of a great diversity of trees.

At some point in Upwood Meadows, you may find yourself being followed by a small herd of pretty cows. Don't be nervous – they are friendly, gentle creatures.

Please close all gates after you, and keep dogs on leads in Upwood Meadows and Lady's Wood.

Route directions

Access the nature reserve through a wooden gate by the grass car park. The detailed information board displays a useful map of the reserve, with its history and wildlife. Go ahead across the meadow. You should see some large anthills, home to yellow meadow ants that only inhabit undisturbed ground. Rabbits are also abundant here.

On reaching the hedge at the far end of the field, cross the stile by a gate and continue ahead. Old shrubs grow in the marshy land to your left. Veer left along a short walk among trees. Cross the stile and go left across the field, heading towards a cluster of trees in the corner. At the end, turn left among the trees. It is a bit boggy here, with an overgrown pond (1) on the left.

Cross the stile on the right, under low, arching trees, and walk ahead across the field. Head left to the stile with a yellow arrow, and pass through a wide old hedge. Keep to the right edge of this meadow. Lady's Wood is ahead. At the field corner, continue ahead between arable fields. The path leads into the ancient wood and curves left at a junction. This wood is a tangled old coppice with a great variety of trees and flowers. Exit the wood at the stile (2), emerging to

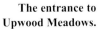

The entrance to Upwood Meadows.

Upwood Meadows' friendly cows.

overlook rolling open countryside with fields, hedges and small woods.

Turn left and follow the woodland edge, then continue ahead at the wood's corner towards a small clump of trees. Past the trees, the path crosses a deep ditch. Go right, following the field edge, then left at the corner to follow a hedge. This path is overgrown and hard going. When you reach a wide track, turn left. At the corner by an old hedge there are a wooden bridge and stile.

Cross the field towards the left corner of the small wood ahead. Pass through the wide gap in the hedge, then cut the corner to the edge of the tree line. Go over the stile on your right. Among the trees to the right are ridges of an old earthwork and moat with water (3).

Walk diagonally across the field towards farm buildings and go through the gap by a stile. Continue ahead, towards the left of a large

27

An overgrown pond.

barn, and cross the stile in the far corner. Follow the short track to a metal gate, go through this and turn left along the wide track for a few steps, then cross the stile on the right. The path passes between tall untidy hedges.

At the end, turn left along the lane into Great Ravelly village. Go left by the post box on to the public footpath, crossing yet another stile. The footpath crosses a strip of land with fruit trees and a dovecote (4), then there is another stile into a field. The track continues ahead, then take the bridge and stile into the next field. The remains of the sail-less Upwood Windmill is visible across the fields to the right. Follow the wire fence along the left edge of the field, then cut the corner to the stile (the path is not obvious, so you could continue following the field edge). Follow the track ahead across this field.

On reaching the road, keep ahead into Upwood village, where the Cross Keys public house, near the village hall, provides rest and refreshment. The church is worth a look, and if you want a short detour on the way back, there is a public footpath behind it, parallel to the road. Opposite the village hall take the public footpath (5), which leads to a road with modern houses. On a bend to the left, there is a public footpath sign on a lamp post to the right. The trail follows mown grass between houses 7 and 9, then crosses a stile into a field.

Cross the field diagonally left to a gap in the far hedge. Turn right, following the hedge along the field edge. Over a bridge and a stile at the far corner, the path leads back into Upwood Meadows Nature Reserve. Turn left back to the car park.

History and Wildlife

Bedfordshire, Cambridgeshire and Northamptonshire Wildlife Trust's Upwood Meadows is a National Nature Reserve and SSSI. This small reserve consists of three fields, with habitats including hedges, scrub, marsh and a pond. One of the fields, Bentley Meadow, has never been treated with herbicide or fertiliser, and the reserve has been grassland for over 280 years. The large anthills of the yellow ant only exist in places that have been undisturbed for many years. Upwood Meadows are especially colourful in May and June, with cowslips and green-winged orchids among the many varieties of wildflowers.

The Wildlife Trust purchased the land in 1977, helped by an anonymous donor and a grant from the World Wide Fund for Nature. This rare and important remnant of Midland clay grassland became a National Nature Reserve in 1981, and is also supported by English Nature, the Countryside Agency, and the Heritage Lottery Fund.

Ridges and furrows in the meadows originate from seventeenth century ploughing. Cows graze the grass each year from April to November.

Places of Interest

The main street of Ramsey used to be a canal, but unfortunately this was filled in and converted into a car park. Ramsey has a rural museum, with exhibits of local agriculture and rural life. This opens Sunday and Thursday afternoons from April to September.

The ruins of Ramsey Abbey lie east of the town.

Walk 4 – OUSE WASHES NATURE RESERVE, MANEA

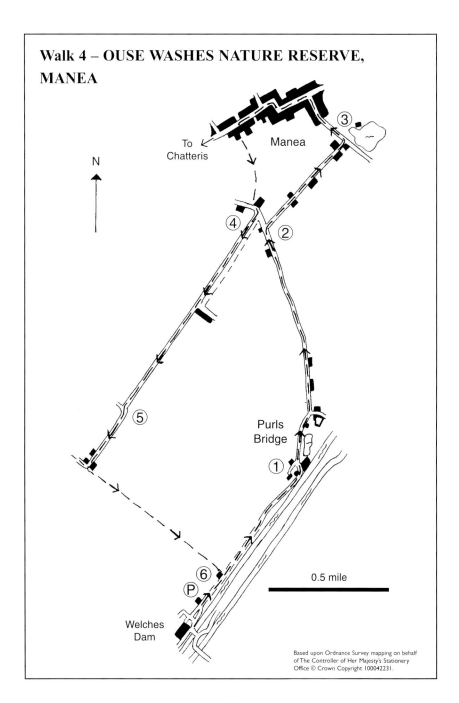

30

Walk 4

OUSE WASHES NATURE RESERVE MANEA

Distance: 5.5 miles

Map: OS Landranger 143

Start/Parking: Car park at the Visitor Centre, Welches Dam; grid ref. TL 472862

Nearest town: Chatteris

LONG straight lines dominate the map of this part of Cambridgeshire, and the parallel Old and New Bedford Rivers are among the longest and straightest features. Most of the 2000 or so hectares of land between the artificial rivers are managed for wildlife conservation. The Ouse Washes Nature Reserve, jointly owned by the Royal Society for the Protection of Birds (RSPB) and the Wildlife Trust for Cambridgeshire, covers 1300 hectares of this.

Because of the shape and limited access to the reserve itself, it was impossible to plan a circular walk at least partly inside the reserve. It is worth going in, though, and exploring the area surrounding Welches Dam pumping station, and visiting Kingfisher Hide with its view over the fens to Ely.

The walk is easy along flat lanes and farm tracks. It was not muddy underfoot when we visited in autumn after a wet spell. There are two stiles. Manea village, about half way round, has the Rose and Crown inn, a general shop and a bench in the churchyard for rest and refreshments.

Route directions

The nature reserve is entered by going over the bridge near Welches Dam pumping station. The first watercourse is a wide dyke, then the Old Bedford River, margined with trees and lush herbage, comes into view on the other side of the embankment. The reserve is popular with anglers as well as bird watchers. What you see on the other side of the river depends on the season and recent weather. For most of the year grazing meadows spread into the distance, but in winter and after wet spells, the land between the Old and New Bedford Rivers is flooded. New Bedford River, over half a mile away, is invisible from here.

Return to the lane and head north away from the Visitor Centre. Soon the road dips and moves slightly away from the dyke. It is easier to walk along the lane, but more interesting to follow the official

Welches Dam pumping station.

footpath on top of the embankment on the right. It is clear that most walkers take the lane, because the footpath is narrow and overgrown with long grasses threaded with meadow weeds. A variety of aquatic plants grow by and in the dyke's clear water. To the left is a wide view over flat, hedgeless fields.

At the public footpath sign the path rejoins the road. Old bushes on the left are smothered with arboreal ivy, with myriad green flower clusters in autumn and black berries in winter. After the ivy is a group of white poplar, the white undersides of its leaves scintillating in the breeze.

At the Ship Inn, Purls Bridge (1), the road bends left away from the dyke and descends gently, passing a pool on the right. After a row of old cottages, young rowans and other trees are growing along the roadside on the left, planted to break the incessant winds.

In the nature reserve we had spotted several dragonflies of different sizes and colours, and here in the lanes they were still prevalent, darting among the long grasses.

The lane drifts away from the Washes, the embankment of which is visible on the right. Ahead left, Manea stands on higher land beyond the fields, an island in an agricultural sea.

Turn right at the junction with Straight Road (2), aptly named because it is dead straight for half a mile. At the end is a pool used for fishing, hidden behind a group of willows. It is worth a little diversion to view it, with its reeds and dragonflies. It is next to a small wood with a rough path leading up a bank to the S M Guy Memorial Playing Field (3). Alternatively you can turn left at the junction and stay with the road into Manea.

The Rose and Crown public house and the village shop are at the end of this road. Turn left and walk past St Nicholas' Church in its peaceful grounds. The road twists between attractive houses and gardens. Take the footpath left between a little shop and the fire station, and go over a stile into a pig farm. The grass trail is clearly marked

Garden in the middle of farmland.

between the enclosures, with electric fences preventing the curious swine from getting too close.

Cross the second stile and turn left along the lane for a short way, then right at the public footpath sign along the Westfield Farms track (4). This is another straight feature, running between fields and occasional farm buildings.

After a mile the track kinks left then right, and here is an unexpected pleasure: a garden (5) with silver birches and a mixture of ornamental shrubs, beautifully tended. This garden is surrounded by open fields and is nowhere near any building. Just past the garden, on the right of the track, there is a rectangular raised reservoir, one of several in the region.

When the track bends right, take the grass track left, following a tree-fringed ditch on your right. Past the trees and in open countryside again, you can see the pump station ahead to the right. The ditch water is clear with the leaves of water hawthorn and other aquatics floating on it.

Turn right at the end by a shed back along the lane to the car park.

History and wildlife

The Visitor Centre is worth investigating. It contains displays about the history, maintenance and wildlife of the reserve, including a spectacular aerial photo of the flooded washes in winter. In fact, winter is the best time for bird watching, when tens of thousands of wildfowl visit the expanse of shallow water. In summer cattle graze the land.

The Ouse Washes are a rare relic of undrained fen, surrounded by drained farmland, which has shrunk and sunk as it dried. Because the farmland is now lower than the rivers passing through it, it is susceptible to flooding.

The Old and New Bedford Rivers meet the Great Ouse River in two places, at Earith in the south-west and Denver near Downham Market in the north-east, cutting straight across a large bend of the Great Ouse. Dutch engineer Cornelius Vermuyden constructed the system in the seventeenth century as part of his great drainage scheme. The Washes act as a giant flood plain to protect over a hundred square miles of farmland and villages. The complex has been modified and improved since it was built. Welches Dam pumping station bears a stone plaque: "Erected by the River Great Ouse Catchment Board 1948".

The parallel drains are nearly twenty miles long, and enclose more than two thousand hectares of water meadows. When water levels rise, due to heavy rainfall or high tides, a system of sluices and pump houses ensures that the enclosed land floods instead of the surrounding countryside. This usually happens in winter, and the site is internationally important for huge flocks of over-wintering waterfowl, including Berwick's swans, teal, pintail, wigeon, shoveler and

Steps up to Kingfisher Hide.

pochard. Several bird hides afford good views across the nature reserve.

In summer the ground is grazed by over two thousand cattle belonging to fifty farmers who rent the summer grazing land from the reserve's owners. The herds are shepherded by RSPB stockmen. The grazing and flooding together prevent bushy vegetation from becoming established, hence preserving the damp meadows and their wildflowers.

The nature reserve contains a number of habitats, including damp grassland, sluggish ditches and the rivers themselves. It supports many rare species such as spined loach fish, red-eyed damselflies, hairy dragonflies and fringed water lilies. It is believed to be the best site in Cambridgeshire for dragonflies, which are noticeable throughout the neighbourhood. Birds that breed here in summer include black-tailed godwits, ruffs, garganeys, spotted crakes, lapwings, redshanks and snipes. The clear water of the ditches and dykes contains water violets, greater water parsnip and other aquatic and marginal plants. More than 260 species of flowering plants have been recorded in the nature reserve.

Places of interest

This region is largely agricultural, but there are a few places nearby worth visiting. Chatteris has Grove House Museum, with collections of local interest (open Thursday afternoons). A few miles north, Stonea Camp is a large Iron Age earthwork in the middle of nowhere.

Walk 5 – ROSWELL PITS, ELY

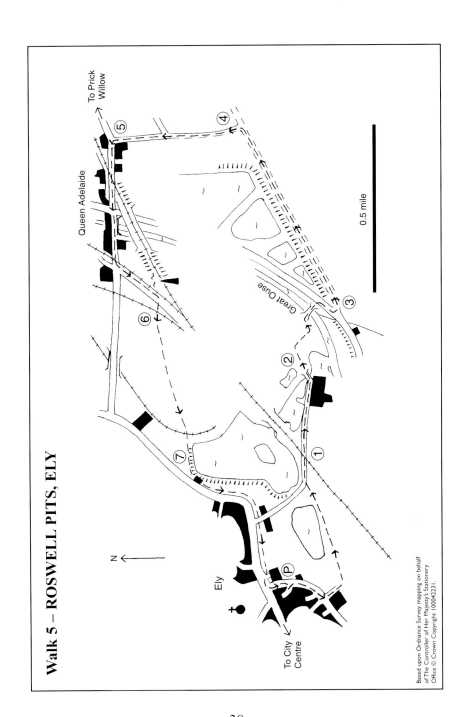

Walk 5

ROSWELL PITS, ELY

Distance: 4.5 miles

Map: OS Landranger 143

Start/Parking: Roswell Drive, Ely, just south of the B1382; grid ref. TL 548806

Nearest town: Ely

THE flooded Roswell Pits, once clay quarries, are now a wildlife oasis in an agricultural desert. The water, reed beds, marsh, meadows, scrub and woods each supports its own ecology, and nature trails with information boards cater for walkers, country lovers – and train enthusiasts. Several busy railway lines network this region, linking at a complicated junction east of Ely.

You could just walk round the flooded pits, but this walk goes further, following the River Ouse for some distance, then returning over farmland, country footpaths and lanes.

Some parts can be extremely muddy after rain, so wear waterproof boots. There are lots of stiles, just when you're starting to get tired, but then you're back on easy tracks and roads. Unfortunately we couldn't find anywhere on route to get food, so it's a good idea to take some sandwiches and a drink.

Banks of flooded pits are steep, so keep away from the edges and stay on the marked nature trails and paths. Dogs should be kept on leads on the nature trails and farm tracks, and by railway lines.

One of the busy railway lines.

Route directions

From Roswell Drive turn right along the road. Flat fields spread for miles on the left. Just after Lisle Close, cross the road and follow the path signed 'The Hereward Way'. This is edged with shrubs and brambles, then small trees coated with mature ivy, its lush black berries valuable for winter birds. Keep ahead at the junction. These paths are well drained, with ditches either side lined with wild arum. The first lake is visible behind trees on the left while, less attractive, to the right is rusting old farm machinery. Quiet electric trains travel the line ahead, frequently. Well-rotted fallen trees, drilled with insect holes of various sizes, have been left to decay naturally.

There is a detour to the lake on the left. This is one of the flooded Roswell Pits, now a wildfowl refuge.

Continue along the nature trail, now margined with mature trees. Tangled woodland fills the space between path and water.

The railway line here (1) is busy, with a train passing every few minutes. Cross when the barriers are raised and walk along Kiln Lane ahead. The low ground to the right is called washland, and is a flood plain to prevent flooding elsewhere. Several bird varieties feed and nest in the rough grass. The River Ouse flows through meadows beyond the washland. Rusty barges float on the flooded pit on the left near the Waterlink buildings.

Go through the wooden gate left of the large metal gates. A sign says: 'Fen Rivers Way', with a picture of an eel.

Cross Cuckoo Bridge (2) over one of the pits. A marble sign tells how: 'Cuckoo Bridge was re-built in year 2000 by Cambridgeshire County Council and the Environment Agency, with funding from East Waste Limited, East Cambridgeshire District Council and the Countryside Agency'. Quite a joint effort. It is an attractive bridge, and from its span there are fine views across the water and country-side.

On the other side there are extensive reed beds left of the path,

41

Old barges on a flooded pit.

which can be muddy here. The track turns sharp right, following a fence, then left to follow the riverbank. Take the metal bridge, ugly compared to Cuckoo Bridge, across the Ouse, then go right along the lane for a little way. Distant Ely Cathedral is visible over fields on the right.

Cross the road and take the concrete track descending to a lane on the left (3). Large, flat fields spread to the right. The lane follows the banks of several flooded pits, but you cannot see the water because its surface is *higher* than the farmland, confined by embankments.

The concrete track turns right, but continue ahead on the dirt track; this is still Hereward Way, as occasional markers point out. A deep drainage ditch on the right is lined with reeds. At an old willow tree (4), take the track to the left, following the 'Rivers Way' marker post. Eventually you reach farm buildings by a road. Turn left along the road and enter Queen Adelaide village over a railway crossing, one of many round here. The road crosses the river over a fine concrete bridge.

Over the next level crossing, go through the gate on the left by a public footpath sign. This path parallels a railway line. Reeds and scrub soon follow houses and gardens on the right. Ely Cathedral lies in the distance behind trees.

Just after a phone mast on the left, take the low bridge with a yellow marker arrow, crossing a ditch on the right. Climb over the high stile, cross the train line with caution, then a second stile (6). The public footpath crosses a field, and the ground can be *very* muddy after rain, believe me. (In fact, it can be so bad that, after a lot of rain, you are advised to take the alternative road route from Queen Adelaide.) Keeping the church spire ahead and slightly to the left, you reach a stile. Cross the next field, then two stiles, another railway, and yet another stile.

Cuckoo Bridge.

43

Roswell Pits lie on the left. Follow the track ahead towards the road, but before reaching the road, take the stile or bridge (7) on the left into a small grassy field. There is a clear, well-trodden path parallel to the road. Cross the lane ahead and go through the gap in the fence into a small grove and across a field. Leave the field at the corner by the road, opposite the cemetery. Turn left and follow the road back to the car park.

History and wildlife

Roswell Pits were dug out over centuries, and the quarried clay used for bricks and strengthening of riverbanks. The heap of excavated clay was called Roswell Hill, but that has all gone now. The area has been designated a Site of Special Scientific Interest to protect fossil beds, laid as deposits in a shallow sea during Jurassic times more than 140 million years ago.

Groundwater has been allowed to flood the depleted pits, and these are now an oasis for wildlife from the surrounding arable farmland. The lakes and river attract wildfowl, and the adjacent reed beds and scrub shelter many birds and insects. Over ninety bird species have been recorded here, including reed and sedge warblers nesting in the reed beds, and kingfishers and cormorants along the river. Water rails and bearded tits visit in winter, and kestrels hunt above the scrub and grassland. Volunteers mow part of the reed beds each winter to prevent them spreading and choking up the water.

The willow trees support more than 450 insect types, including the rare musk beetle whose larvae burrow into young branches. Orchids and other flowers grow in the meadows. The grass is kept clear of scrub so wildflowers can flourish, visited by hosts of bees and butter-flies.

The site is owned by the National Rivers Authority and managed by the Wildlife Trust for Cambridgeshire.

Places of interest

The city of Ely, with its huge cathedral known as the 'Ship of the Fens', was once an island surrounded by marshland. The cathedral dominates the flat landscape for miles around. Ely has an attractive riverside, where you can hire a boat or walk along the banks.

Oliver Cromwell lived in the Steward's House at Ely for ten years from 1636, when he took over from his grandfather as Steward, or tythe-farmer, of the Dean and Chapter of Ely. During the Civil War, Cromwell ordered Canon Hitch, who was responsible for the cathedral services, to repent from his popish ways. The Canon ignored Cromwell, who then led a body of soldiers into the cathedral during Holy Communion and drove out clergy and congregation.

Cromwell's house, 29 St Mary's Street, has been refurbished as a museum of seventeenth century life, and includes an exhibition on the drainage of the Fens. Ely Tourist Information is also housed in this building.

Ely Museum, in the Old Gaol, Market Street, tells the history of the Isle of Ely from the last Ice Age to the present. Ely Stained Glass Museum at the Cathedral contains a national collection of stained glass from medieval to modern.

South-east of Ely, Soham has a working windmill producing various types of flour, and is open on Sundays and bank holiday Mondays. At Stretham to the south of Ely, there is a giant parallel beam engine built in 1831 for draining the surrounding fens.

Walk 6 – PAXTON PITS NATURE RESERVE

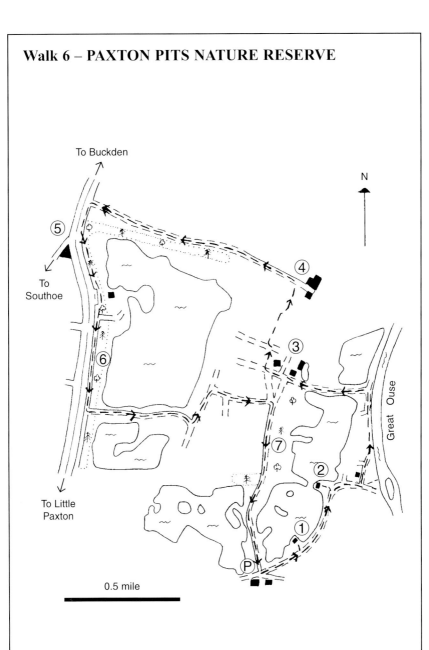

To Buckden

N

To Southoe

To Little Paxton

Great Ouse

0.5 mile

Walk 6

PAXTON PITS NATURE RESERVE

Distance: 4 miles

Map: OS Landranger 153

Start/Parking: Paxton Pits Nature Reserve car park, Little Paxton; grid ref. TL 195629

Nearest towns: St Neots

WE chose to visit Paxton Pits in winter because large areas of water often attract migratory waterfowl. We were not disappointed. A variety of birds were flying, swimming, or making a cacophony on the islands.

This local nature reserve and Site of Scientific Interest also appeals to plant lovers, with spring and summer wildflowers adorning the clearings and meadow areas. The flooded gravel pits alongside the River Great Ouse are surrounded by mature willows, oaks and other trees reflecting in the water, making this a very picturesque site.

The Visitor Centre near the car park opens on Sundays, more often in summer, and provides refreshments and toilets. It has leaflets showing maps and nature trail routes (also available from St Neots Tourist Information office). Our route is slightly longer than these and leaves the reserve for a while to explore the surrounding fields and woods.

Paths are excellent, especially in the reserve, and there is very little mud even during a wet winter. Many of the paths and one of the bird hides are suitable for wheelchairs. Dogs are welcome in the reserve if kept under control. There is one stile on this walk. Visitors are warned never to swim in the flooded pits and to keep an eye on children and dogs; the pools are deep with steep sides.

Route directions

Before setting off, look at the information board in the car park with a map of the nature reserve and some of the creatures who live here. The Visitor Centre, whether open or not, has more information boards on its outside walls, and a small wildlife pond and picnic area.

Cross the wooden footbridge by the car park and follow the path ahead. This curves round the left of a low mound and passes a decidedly non-native clump of pampas grass, its tall feathery blooms waving in the breeze. The vegetation round here is briar scrub, with pink roses in summer and large red hips in winter. There are bird boxes high on the sparse trees and dead telegraph poles, their wires long gone.

Cross the road and go through the kissing gate. Heronry South Pit, the oldest flooded gravel pit, is visible through the trees to your left. Soon Hayden Hide (1) appears by the water. Between the path and the hide, behind a recently planted hedgerow, is an open area that was once a store for excavated sand and gravel. The ground is too poor for grass and most other plants, but is covered with a mosaic of green, yellow and grey mosses.

Heronry South Pit.

Hayden Hide was won in a competition run by Bird Watching magazine, and erected with help from Huntingdonshire District Council. It was dedicated to the memory of Derek Hayden, a long serving Quarry Manager with Aggregate Industries, and opened in April 1997. The hide gives an excellent view across the lake. You will probably hear the wildfowl before you see them: chattering herons and cormorants roost on the islands.

Kingfisher Hide.

Continue along the path by the lake. To the right is boggy grassland, with mosses and sedges dominant in the wetter parts, and teasels in the drier parts. To stop hawthorn, dog rose and bramble scrub encroaching, these bushes are regularly cut back, allowing the rough, wet grassland to thrive as a valuable habitat. Some massive logs have been set on either side of the path, with interesting bracket fungi growing out of their ends. Heaps of smaller logs support various fungi and mosses.

Just before reaching the turn-off to Kingfisher Hide, you may notice some plants normally seen in gardens, like lavender and periwinkle. A Victorian dwelling called Wray House used to stand here, and these plants, popular with butterflies, moths and goldcrests, are the remains of its garden.

Divert left to Kingfisher Hide (2), at the end of a peninsular covered with mature oaks. This hide affords great views over the water of Heronry South and North Pits.

Return to the path and follow it as it bends right towards the river. It then turns left and approaches boat moorings on the river. This path is part of the Ouse Valley Way long distance path, a twenty-six mile riverside walk linking Earith and St Neots. In the 18th century, a ferry here linked Little Paxton with Great Paxton (now the smaller of the two villages) across the river.

The path cuts through a thicket of bramble and hawthorn, with ancient willows covered with ivy. These trees and ivy are an important wildlife haven, supporting more than two hundred and fifty varieties of insects. At the junction turn left and walk between Heronry North Pit on your left and Washout Pit on your right. Common terns nest along the sandy margins of Washout Pit in summer. Common spotted orchids grow around here, their dark pink spires appearing in summer.

Leave the nature reserve and continue ahead past the gravel works (3), keeping to the marked paths. There is an information board showing what the quarry machines do, the pits' history, and what the excavated sand and gravel are used for. Quarrying began in the 1930s to

Log seat.

50

provide hardcore for airfield runways. Today the sand and gravel are used locally for building.

Cross the road, looking out for lorries, and continue ahead, then turn right. The trail bends left then, after a short distance, take the narrow grass footpath on the right. This leads between shrubs and trees, including a small plantation of young ashes, to the attractive farmhouse and wooden barns of Boughton Lodge Farm (4). Turn left along the track towards the A1. On the left is an arable field. Rough shrubby pasture lies to the right, beyond which stands the chunky spire of Buckden church nearly four miles away.

Soon a narrow band of trees parallels the track beyond the field on the left, a windbreak of deciduous trees and cylindrical conifers. The track ends at the busy A1, where fortunately there is an excellent footpath. Turn left and, after a short distance, left again at the Public Footpath sign just before the Southoe junction (5). Climb the stile and follow the path through the tree belt by the roadside.

At the field edge the path turns right and follows the trees parallel to the road, then joins a long straight track bordered by narrow woodland. More cylindrical conifers stand amongst the broad-leaved trees. Bordering the lane (6) is what appears to be an overgrown hedge of *Lonicera nitida*, a small leaved evergreen commonly grown in garden hedgerows. The presence of these non-native trees and shrubs suggests that this region was once part of a large garden or estate driveway.

At the junction take the path left between two large flooded pits. The left lake spreads scenically behind a thin line of trees. The right pit is invisible behind young hedging and other vegetation. At the end turn left, then right towards the gravel works. Re-enter the nature reserve and turn right along the lane between mixed woodland (watch out for lorries). To the left is a large conservation area (7) not open to the public: a mix of woodland, scrub and grassland. When the road emerges near the Visitor Centre, turn right back to the car park.

History and wildlife

Detailed information on the history, quarrying and wildlife conservation at Paxton Pits is available at the excellent web site www.paxton-pits.org.uk.

The area that is now Paxton Pits has a complex geological history, and fossils of sea creatures dating from 480 million years ago have been found here. Over the eons the region alternated between land and shallow sea where rivers and sea movements deposited sand and gravel.

Excavation of gravel and sand began in earnest in the 1930s for airfield runways construction, became more extensive after World War 2, and continues today to the north of the reserve. The pits in the nature reserve were dug between the 1940s and the early 1960s. These flooded pits and their surroundings now support many waterfowl, wetland wildflowers and insects.

Paxton Pits was designated a Local Nature Reserve in 1988, and was opened officially in June 1989. Redland Aggregates provided the Visitor Centre, which is staffed by volunteer wardens. The nature reserve, consisting of 147 acres west of the River Great Ouse, is managed by Huntingdonshire District Council's Countryside Services with help from local volunteers. Its flooded excavations are the main habitat, but there are also reed beds, damp meadows, scrub, woodland, and the river. Many birds live by or visit the lakes, including geese, tufted ducks, moorhens, mallards and coots. Most obvious are the noisy herons and cormorants living on the islands – Paxton's cormorant breeding colony is England's second largest. During our walk a heron flew low overhead, calling loudly – a most impressive bird. You may spot a kingfisher along the river. The reed beds are important nesting sites for reed warblers, mute swans and great crested grebes.

The woodland clearings and meadows are colourful with wildflowers in summer, attracting brimstone, tortoiseshell and other butterflies. Dragonflies and damselflies flit around the water edges.

The lakes have been stocked with roach, tench and carp, making them popular with anglers. The lake margins and damp meadows support many wetland wildflowers, including yellow flag irises, willow herbs and common spotted orchids, and white willows line the lakes and river.

The reserve contains large thickets of hawthorn, bramble and dog rose scrub. These provide cover for nesting birds, their flowers attract insects in early summer, and birds and small mammals eat their colourful fruits in autumn and winter. Although a valuable habitat, scrub spreads and smothers grassland if left, so parts have to be cut back at times to keep it under control.

Places of interest

St Neots is an attractive small town with a museum, a Tuesday market, St Mary's parish church with an ornate tower dominating this part of the Ouse valley, and over two hundred buildings of historical or architectural interest. Its market square, normally used as a car park, contains an unusual lamp stand called the Day Column. Erected in 1822 by local brewer John Day, this once dispensed water piped from the local spa.

Buckden village, north of Paxton Pits, has lots of old buildings, shops and pubs. Buckden Towers, the Bishop of Lincoln's palace in Tudor times, is where Queen Catherine of Aragon, Henry VIII's first wife, was imprisoned from 1533 until their divorce in 1534. The fifteenth century gatehouse and Great Tower remain. In the grounds is a walled garden set out in Tudor style and dedicated to Queen Catherine.

Grafham Water, west of Buckden, is a large Anglian Water reservoir formed in the 1960s by damming Diddington Brook (see Walk 2: Brampton Wood, for more details).

Walk 7 – WARESLEY AND GRANSDEN WOODS

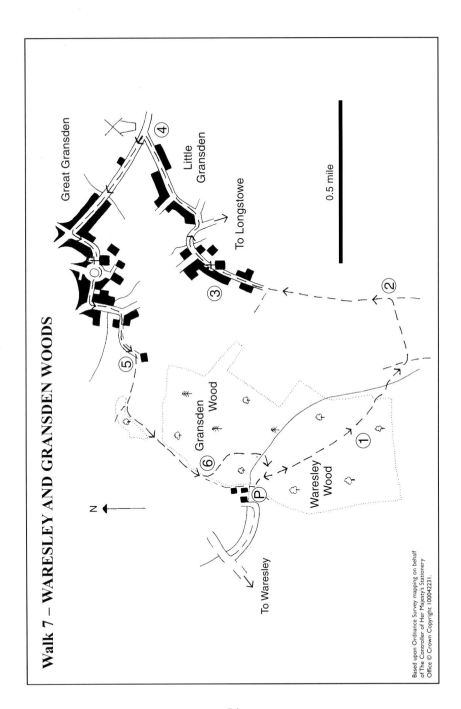

0.5 mile

Walk 7

WARESLEY AND GRANSDEN WOODS

Distance: 3.5 miles

Map: Landranger 153

Start/Parking: Car park at Waresley and Gransden Woods;
                    grid ref. TL 259550

Nearest town: St Neots

THIS walk begins by exploring the ancient Waresley and Gransden Woods. These adjoining woods are coppiced with standards, and are an important conservation site for rare woodland flowers and creatures. They have been designated a Site of Special Scientific Interest.

Emerging from the woods, the trail then crosses fields and enters the attractive villages of Little and Great Gransden, each with its own public house, before returning to the woods.

There are a few stiles, and some paths can be muddy at times. Dogs are not allowed in Waresley and Gransden Woods. Visitors should keep to the marked trails in the woods.

Route directions

Cross the wooden bridge over a ditch and enter the woods. An information board with a map tells about the history, wildlife and management of these ancient woods. Follow the long straight ride ahead. The woodland beyond the ditch to the right is boggy, and there are hazel coppice and a pool to the left.

Soon you come across an unusual shelter made from branches (1). If you stand here quietly and look out the windows, you may spot tree

**Ornate wooden
shelter, Waresley
Wood.**

creepers, small birds that walk spirally up tree trunks looking for insects and spiders to eat. The hazel stools around the shelter are ancient: huge and crooked, covered with moss and ivy, sprouting new branches.

Continue ahead. The path leaves the wood and enters a field. Fork left and follow the ditch on the left, then turn left and cross the ditch. A hawthorn and sloe hedge borders the left side of the path, with an arable field to the right. Go left at the marker post by a large hawthorn (2). Hedgerows, with occasional mature trees, margin this track. Cowslips and forget-me-nots bloom here in spring and early summer.

Eventually you reach the outskirts of Little Gransden village. There are some interesting buildings and gardens here, including a large house with a duck pond in its garden (3), a thatched house with a thatch squirrel on the roof, and some topiary conifers.

The stone square tower of Little Gransden church soon appears on the right. Follow the road ahead at the junction by a bus shelter. From the stream bridge, Great Gransden church tower is visible to the left. Turn left at Primrose Hill; the lane ascends past more pretty houses and gardens.

Great Gransden post mill.

Where the lane leaves the village, Great Gransden Mill stands proudly ahead left. A sign informs that this post mill was built in the seventeenth century and last worked in 1911. It was restored in 1982–83, financed in part by Great Gransden Village Society. Post mills are common in Cambridgeshire and Suffolk; the whole building turns so that the sails face into wind, as opposed to the more usual arrangement of just the top part turning.

Gransden lodge marker stone.

A plaque on a nearby stone (4) marks an entrance to Gransden Lodge, now the site of Cambridge Gliding Club. It was an RAF airfield during World War 2.

Follow the lane to the left, descending towards Great Gransden. Go left at Church Street; St Bartholomew's tower is visible ahead. The church has an interesting lych gate, erected in 1920 as a war memorial.

At the tiny roundabout, take the exit to Crow Tree Street, then left at the end. Across the stream, take the public footpath to the right, leaving the village. There is rough pasture on the left, and to the right a meadow behind straggly trees slopes down to the stream. At the white gate (5), take the narrow path to the right and cross the stile. Gransden Wood is visible beyond the field on the left. The path follows the right edge of the field by a row of trees, obviously an old hedgerow, and then curves to meet the wood's corner. Cross the ditch between trees on the right and follow the woodland edge. There is a good view across the gently rolling countryside to the right, with its fields and trees. Waresley church spire is visible above the trees ahead.

Enter the wood at the stile (6) on the left. Fork right at the junction. The path descends to a stream, crossed by a wooden bridge. Fork right and return to the car park.

History and wildlife

Waresley and Gransden Woods are ancient, and could be a rare surviving remnant of the wildwood that colonised Britain after the retreat of the last Ice Age ten thousand years ago. For centuries it was coppiced to provide a constant supply of timber and fuel. Oak and ash trees were left to grow as standards. The Domesday Book mentions these woods as coppice.

Most woods were cleared after World War 2 for agricultural land. Part of Waresley Wood was lost between 1947 and 1973, and much of Gransden Wood was felled and replaced with plantations.

Bedfordshire and Cambridgeshire Wildlife Trust owns about half of Waresley Wood and leases the rest, together with part of Gransden Wood. The tradition of coppicing is maintained, allowing spring flowers to thrive in the resulting open woodland. Oxlips, greater butterfly orchid, bluebells, primroses, bugle and wood anemone grow here. Parts of the wood grow on chalky boulder clay, while others are on acidic greensand, with different trees and wildflowers found on the different soils.

As with most woods managed for wildlife, dead trees and log piles are left for habitats.

Places of interest

Another post mill stands near Bourn, a few miles north-east of Waresley and Gransden Woods. Thought to be the oldest post mill in England, it was built in 1636. Owned and maintained by the Cambridge Preservation Society, the mill is open to the public on the last Sunday of each month in summer.

Bourn church is unusual in having a maze on the tower floor. Church mazes were widespread once, but only a few remain.

The town of St Neots, a few miles west of the Gransdens, is described in Walk 6, Paxton Pits Nature Reserve.

Walk 8 – FOWLMERE NATURE RESERVE

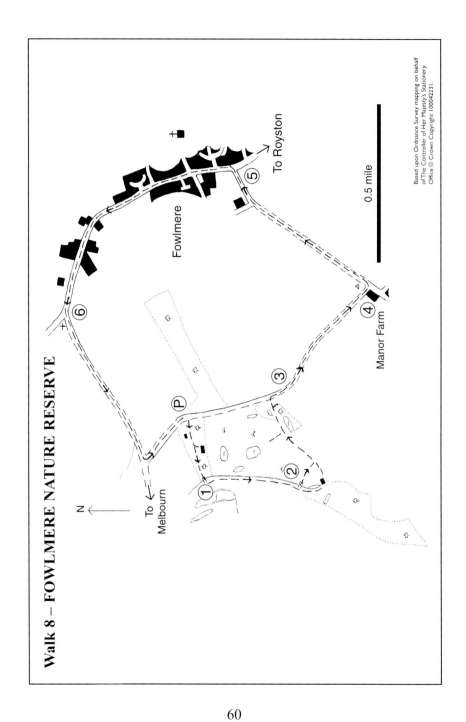

Based upon Ordnance Survey mapping on behalf of The Controller of Her Majesty's Stationery Office © Crown Copyright 100042231.

Walk 8

FOWLMERE NATURE RESERVE

Distance: Four miles

Map: OS Landranger 154

Start/Parking: Fowlmere Nature Reserve car park;
                   grid ref. TL 408459

Nearest towns: Melbourn, Royston (Bedfordshire)

THE Royal Society for the Protection of Birds (RSPB) nature reserve is an oasis of rare wet woodland in an agricultural landscape. Although the site is managed primarily to attract birds, by its nature it also supports all sorts of other creatures and plants. The wood is particularly colourful in spring and early summer, when the hawthorn, roses and other shrubs bloom, and in autumn when they produce their luscious berries. We did this walk in autumn, and I have never seen such a rich display of guelder rose and other fruits. There are also extensive reedbeds and some meadow areas.

After meandering through the nature reserve with its many habitats, the walk leaves the wood to cross open fields with views over the rolling countryside, passes through Fowlmere village, and returns via pleasant lanes.

Birds are not the only things to take to the skies round here. Historic planes from the nearby Imperial War Museum at Duxford, and more modern light aircraft from Fowlmere Aerodrome, are often airborne, joined in calm weather by hot air balloons.

Dogs are not allowed in the nature reserve. Paths are very good and there are no stiles or steps. The chalk soil is well drained although after rain there may be a little mud in places. There are several seats by the route.

Woodland picnic area.

Route directions

Enter the reserve across the wooden bridge over a ditch. Go ahead, following the 'Nature trail and hides' sign. There is a picnic area to the right, surrounded by willow, ash and hawthorn trees, and by the path are information boards about the history and wildlife of the reserve.

Soon the path becomes a boardwalk. Turn left at the junction, following the sign to Drewer Hide. This part of the wood is mainly young trees and shrubs: guelder rose, hawthorn, privet, buckthorn, wild rose and alder, with ivy covering some of the trees. There are open meadow areas with seeds left on willow herbs and other plants for seed-eating birds.

The wooden hide ahead was built in memory of Carl Drewer, 1970–1985, 'Who loved nature all his life'. Inside are some information posters, and viewing windows overlooking a large pool with reedbeds. The clear water supports many aquatic plants.

Retrace the path a little way and take the narrower path on the right. This winds between trees, and there are fallen trees, logs and log piles lying around, some new, some rotting away nicely. The path then follows the woodland edge, with fields visible behind the trees and ditch to the right. The hawthorn trees here have obviously been coppiced, with multiple trunks. On the right by the ditch is an ancient willow: its main trunk is growing horizontally, rooting where it touches the ground, with thick branches growing upwards.

The path crosses a wooden bridge (1) over an incredibly clear stream. A variety of plants grow in the crystal water, and chalk bedrock is visible below. The trail follows the stream bank between reedbeds, then shrubs. One huge willow has a low horizontal branch making a natural bridge over the stream; it has a bird box high on its main trunk. A little further on, a large old man's beard (*Clematis*

Bridge over a clear stream.

63

vitalbe), mixed with ivy, is draped over hawthorn and other shrubs to the right.

Cross the bridge on your left (2) over the stream. The trail crosses a large area of sedge. Turn left at the track ahead, following a wire fence on the right. Cross a wide water channel and continue ahead; there are side-paths to two more bird hides if you are interested in further diversions. Ignore the board walk to the left and continue ahead towards a five-bar gate (3). Go through the gap on the right of the gate.

Turn right and go through the metal gate towards Manor Farm. There is a small airfield, Fowlmere Aerodrome, beyond the farm ahead. This path leaves the wood and hedges behind, rising gently between undulating open fields. The higher you go, the more spectacular is the view, and at the top of the ridge it is well worth stopping to have a good look round, especially behind towards the nature reserve. On a clear day, smoke from the tall chimney at Barningham cement works is visible, and you may see the Staughton radio mast twenty miles away near Grafham Water.

The dirt track becomes concrete. On the left is a small plantation of young trees, and on the right is a memorial stone (4). During the war the 339th Fighter Group of the 8th Airforce flew Mustangs off the grass runway at Manor Farm.

Turn left at the end of the track and follow the lane away from Manor Farm. There is an OS triangulation post on the left verge of this lane. Down in the valley to the right, traffic on the busy A505 can be seen - and heard!

Leave Manor Farm through the gateway (5) at the lane end and turn left along High Street, Fowlmere. There is a choice of public houses in the village centre: the Queen's Head and the Swan House Inn, both of which serve food.

Continue ahead down Long Lane, then turn left at Mill Road (6), following the RSPB sign; there is a small cemetery with chapel on the

Memorial plaque, Manor Farm.

far corner. The track to the nature reserve is on the left, about half a mile along the lane.

History and wildlife

Once much of this region was wet woodland, but most has been converted to farmland. The RSPB purchased Fowlmere reserve in 1977, with money raised by the Young Ornithologist's Club, the junior branch of the RSPB. As a consequence, children are especially welcome to visit the reserve, and educational trips by schools and other groups can be arranged.

Centuries ago, this mixture of damp wood, reedbeds and meadows was a huge lake where people hunted ducks and snipes. It gradually silted up to form marshland with reedbeds and ponds. Locals cut the reeds for thatching, and collected leeches for hospitals and edible frogs for food. Watercress was grown from 1890 to 1980 in the pure water emerging from chalk springs. The water is still very pure and supports a diversity of aquatic plants.

Fowlmere Nature Reserve is a rare wetland, important for many types of birds as well as other creatures and plants. It needs continuous maintenance to prevent silting up and conversion of the whole site to woodland. Birds resident here include moorhens, ducks, water rails and kingfishers, with reed and sedge warblers nesting in the reedbeds. Cuckoos visit in summer, laying their eggs in other birds' nests. In winter, redwings and fieldfares feed from the berried shrubs and roost in the tangled branches. Sparrowhawks hunt here.

Aquatic insects inhabit the pools, including types of dragonflies and damselflies, great diving beetles, and rare water stick insects.

Some clearings are mown as flower meadows, supporting cowslips in spring, orchids in summer, and devil's bit scabious in autumn, among other varieties. These attract butterflies and other insects, including brimstone butterflies. Seedheads are left in autumn and winter for finches and other seed-eating birds.

Otters returned here in 1997, after a twenty year absence.
The reserve contains a two mile nature trail, most of which is followed as part of this walk.

Places of interest

Fowlmere village is proud of its history, and has its own web site (fowlmerevillage.com) to tell you about it. The oldest feature is the Round Moat, an ancient landmark which is the remains of a ninth century Saxon settlement. In fact this whole region is rich in remains from the Iron Age and Roman and Saxon times.

The Imperial War Museum, Duxford, is worth a visit while you are in the region, whether or not there is an air show going on. On non-show days, often one or more of the collection's wartime aircraft takes to the skies, or a more modern one flies in to land. It is easy to spend several hours there, looking round the hangars with their displays of vintage planes, tanks, artillery and military vehicles. The newest building is the American Air Museum, designed by Sir Norman Foster, western end of the site; there is a little railway to take you to it if you don't want the long walk – especially after trekking round Fowlmere Reserve and village!

The small town of Melbourn straddles the A10 London to Cambridge road. It has a fine church, some of which dates back to the thirteenth century, with additions built on during the fourteenth and fifteenth centuries.

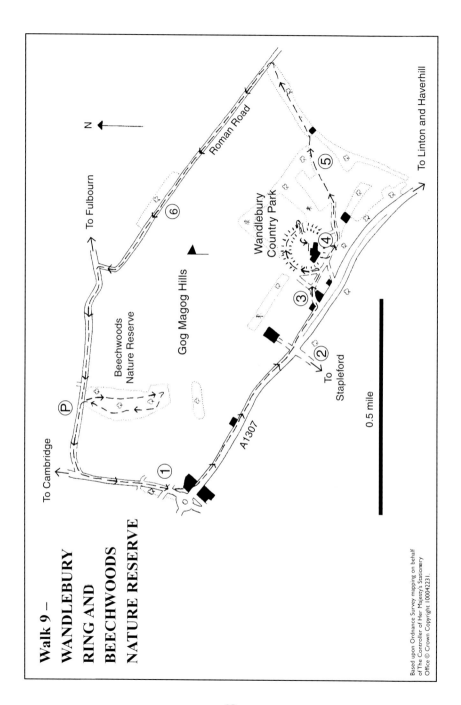

Walk 9 –
WANDLEBURY
RING AND
BEECHWOODS
NATURE RESERVE

To Cambridge

To Fulbourn

N

Roman Road

Beechwoods
Nature Reserve

Gog Magog Hills

Wandlebury
Country Park

To Linton and Haverhill

To
Stapleford

A1307

0.5 mile

Walk 9

WANDLEBURY RING AND BEECHWOODS NATURE RESERVE

Distance   6 miles

Map: OS Landranger 154

Start/Parking: Lay-by next to Beechwoods Local Nature Reserve; grid ref. TL 485548

Nearest town: Cambridge

THIS interesting part of Cambridgeshire is rich in wildlife habitats. Even the roadside verges contain a plethora of wildflowers and grasses. This walk includes two small nature reserves and the curious remains of an Iron Age hill fort.

Beechwoods Local Nature Reserve is well worth investigating; this small wood has old and new halves, each with a very different character. Wandlebury Ring earthworks and estate have a long, interesting history. Wandlebury Country Park includes the recently established Clarks' Corner Nature Reserve, with copses and meadowland.

The chalk soil in this region is well drained, so mud is unlikely to hamper your progress. Paths are generally good. Dogs should be kept on leads in the nature reserves and Wandlebury estate.

Route directions

Cross the road and enter Beechwoods Nature Reserve at the sign, via a few steps, a stile and a gate on the right. A board contains a map and information about the history and nature of this small wood. There is a choice of routes among the trees. The left fork takes you through

69

established woodland dominated by large beech. The shaded, dry ground supports little flora, but there are some unusual mosses.

All paths converge at the old wood's south-east corner. Go through the gate here and fork right into young woodland. The trees are growing in a matrix of long grass and meadow flowers. The path leads downhill back towards the road. Addenbrooke's Hospital dominates the view, beyond fields ahead.

Leave the nature reserve through the entrance gate and turn left along the lane. There is a bramble thicket on the left verge, and undulating fields to the right are visible through gaps in the mixed hedgerow. Turn left at the junction, signed to Shelford. This is quite a busy road, but you can walk on the verge most of the way. Gog Magog Golf Course (1) is ahead left, its strange name taken from the Gog Magog Hills on which it stands. These 'hills' are merely large undulations, slightly higher than the surrounding countryside.

Just before the roundabout, fork left to cut the corner and follow the decent path alongside the duel carriageway. Magog Down (2), a treecrowned knoll, is visible ahead right. Past a farm shop, the road rises and the path becomes a wide grass verge. At the top of the slope, go left through the gates by the sign: 'Public footpath to Wandlebury Ring and Roman Road'. On the other side of the gateway is a bungalow with an immaculate garden. The small building on the left is the Philip Clarke Lecture Room, built in memory of the Cambridge Preservation Society's honorary secretary, 1975–1977.

Continue along the wide track, following the sign. After a few metres, you come to an open area of long grass with several beehives, behind a spaced row of copper birch left of the track (3). On the right there is a wood yard, with a huge circular saw and log piles. A short distance further on, a small stone concrete marker, circular with a conical top, stands to the left. Mature trees meet overhead. The track curves right.

When you reach the road to Wandlebury car park, there is an information board about Wandlebury Country Park estate. Take the path left towards Wandlebury Ring. It curves left around some brick buildings, then right to circumnavigate the Ring. The path follows the ditch between the inner and outer embankments. The vegetation here is trees with dense understorey. Continue ahead at the crossroad. The path descends and undulates among large yews. There are occasional entrances to the Ring interior on the right.

In the ditch of Wandlebury Ring.

Tadlow Granary.

At the arched brick bridge over the path, climb up the left bank and cross the bridge into the Ring. There is another information board here, telling the Ring's history. On the left is a small timber building on stout brick stilts: Tadlow Granary. This was once part of a group of farm buildings at Tadlow in south-west Cambridgeshire. At a cost of £20,000, funded partly by grants, the granary was carefully dismantled and re-erected here.

Turn left towards the hall, across the lawn with a central sundial. The grand building is Gog Magog House, the main part of which was built in the eighteenth century with several later extensions. Once there were stables here that housed racehorses. Above the hall's pedimented archway is a cupola with an ornate eighteenth century clock, restored in 1977. The clock's faces, on each of the four sides of the cupola, are of the old one-handed type. The house has been converted

72

Gog Magog House.

in part to private houses and apartments, and walkers are asked to be quiet and considerate to the occupants.

Walk along the front of the building. The Cambridge Protection Society has its headquarters here. A small information centre has displays and leaflets, mainly about events held at the estate, and toilets. Go through the arch. On the right is a wall plaque stating that Terence Gray, in memory of his parents' association with the Gog Magog estates, gave the land and buildings within Wandlebury Ring to the Cambridge Protection Society in 1954. Among the cobbles at the foot of the wall lies a large slab inscribed: 'The Godolphon Arabian, died in 1753, aged 29'.

The archway leads to a courtyard. Leave this between the brick pillars on the right. Immediately on the right, a flight of five stone steps, covered with mosses and lichens, leads nowhere.

The track curves left and returns to the lane by the car park. Turn left along this lane. After a bench on the left, there is a fenced off pond (4) which is being improved to support more wildlife. Frogs and toads are rare in this region because of lack of standing water.

The lane curves left again to a bridge into the estate, but take the right fork between two wooden posts, following the arrow. There is a picnic and play area on the right. Among the benches here, there is a particularly attractive one with a carved rose.

The wide grass path enters a wood. Fork left at the marker post, following the arrow. The meadow on the right is part of the Clarks' Corner Nature Reserve (5). The path narrows by the edge of a beech wood on the left. At the north end of Clarks' Corner, the trail passes between two concrete pillars and bends left. The extensive golf course spreads to the left. At the sign "Public Footpath to Roman Road", take the left path into shady beech woodland. The ground is spongy underfoot from decades of leafmould and beech masts. It is quiet here, apart from the breeze in the treetops and singing birds. The trail ahead is dead straight.

Turn left on to the Roman road, now just a straight path between tall trees and hedges. In summer there are many wild flowers in the verges, including unusual white knapweed among the normal purple flowers. The path ascends slowly. There is a dark stretch under arching trees (6). It ends at a small car park. Follow the wider track to the right, then turn left along the lane. There is a great view over the fields to Cambridge beyond. You can walk on the right verge, which is gorgeous with wildflowers in summer. Beechwoods Nature Reserve's band of trees is visible ahead.

History and wildlife

This region of Cambridgeshire is called the Gog Magog Hills. It is an outcrop of the chalk upfold that includes the Chilterns, Dunstable Downs, Therfield Heath and Royston. Its natural history is characteristic of chalk downs.

Beechwoods Local Nature Reserve is mostly young woodland. The beech, ash, yew, crab apple and field maple were planted in 1991, with the help of a Forestry Authority Grant. Skylarks, partridges and peasants nest and feed in the long grass amongst the young trees. Eventually this area will grow into a fine mixed wood. The reserve is already supporting woodland birds such as tits and warblers. Butterflies and other insects service the wildflowers in the network of glades and rides.

The eastern strip of woodland is much older, and consists mainly of beech planted in 1840. It contains a series of flat, wide terraces: the remains of medieval plough strips. Mosses and woodland flowers grow in the dry ground beneath the trees, including the rare white helleborine orchid which flowers in June and July. The old wood is managed by thinning and replanting with ash, field maple, hawthorn and yew to increase the variety and age of the trees. Fungi grow on dead tree stumps and fallen trunks.

Wandlebury estate includes Wandlebury Ring and Country Park. In 1954, the then owner Terence Gray donated most of the land and buildings to the Cambridge Protection Society (CPS), in memory of his parents Sir Harold and Lady Edwina Gray. The CPS drew on their 'Save the Gogs Fund', set up in 1937, to buy the remainder of the estate and save it from development. Maintenance is expensive, and grants from the Countryside Commission, Forestry Commission and various local councils have helped with this, although donations are always welcome.

Wandlebury Ring, the remains of an Iron Age fort, is three hundred metres in diameter. It consists of two concentric embankments separated by a two and a half metre ditch. In the Ring's centre is a dew pond, probably dug by the Iron Age occupants to collect water. It is cleaned out regularly to prevent it silting up.

Beehives, near Wandlebury Ring.

76

Sheep grazed the site in the middle ages. Trees were planted in the late sixteenth and early eighteenth centuries to provide cover for hunting and shooting. Wandlebury estate is now an important nature conservation site, with over two hundred flower species listed, including spring bulbs, woodland wildflowers and garden escapees. Lots of different types of fungi live in the woods and meadows, including wood blewit, beefsteak, deadman's fingers, earth star and parasol. The estate supports many woodland birds, mammals and insects.

The small Clarks' Nature Reserve in Wandlebury Country Park was established in 1998 by the Woodland Trust as a result of a local appeal. Named after Bill and Wendy Clark, who managed Wandlebury estate for over twenty-five years, it contains newly planted trees and chalk grassland flora.

Places of interest

If you still have energy left after this long, interesting walk, or just need a sit down and a coffee, Cambridge centre is less than four miles drive from Beechwoods Nature Reserve. I strongly recommend using a park-and-ride from the outskirts.

Cambridge is a fine city with lots of historical buildings. The University colleges, some of which are fantastic buildings, dominate the centre; the earliest colleges were founded in the fourteenth century. There are bookshops to die for, and miscellaneous museums. Cambridge's botanical gardens are, in my view, even more interesting and educational than the larger ones at Kew. And if you are feeling adventurous, you could try your hand at punting on the River Cam.

Walk 10 – CHIPPENHAM FEN NATURE RESERVE

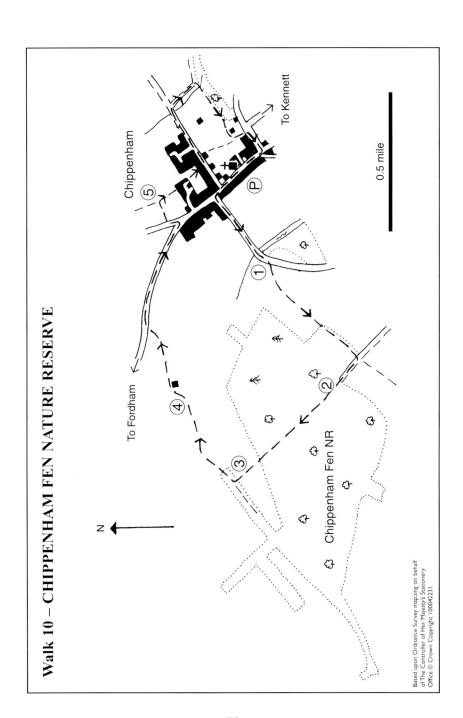

N

Chippenham

To Kennett

To Fordham

Chippenham Fen NR

0.5 mile

Walk 10

CHIPPENHAM FEN NATURE RESERVE

Distance: 4 miles

Map: OS Landranger 154

Start/Parking: Lay-by at St Margaret's Church, Chippenham; grid ref. TL 664698

Nearest town: Newmarket

CHIPPENHAM Fen National Nature Reserve is very boggy, a rare remnant of Cambridgeshire fen. It consists of marshland, reedbeds and damp woodland. Fortunately the public footpath leading through the reserve's centre is relatively dry, although it can still get muddy in places. We did this walk in early January when the mud was frozen solid, which was a good idea, we thought. English Nature's web site suggests that May to July is the best time to visit the reserve for wild-flowers – but wear your waterproof boots just in case.

Chippenham is an attractive village. Being near Newmarket with its famous stud and racetrack, it is hardly surprising that lots of horses live around here in fields and paddocks. There are some unusual and attractive semi-detached houses near Chippenham estate, painted red or yellow with massive front gardens.

Chippenham Fen is privately owned and leased by English Nature. Visitors are asked to keep to the public footpath and not stray into the reserve, and keep their dogs on leads.

Route directions

Head north past the phone box. An interesting small shelter with an old pump stands at the corner of Palace Lane. Go left along this lane,

This region is famous for horses.

following the mellow brick boundary wall of Chippenham Park estate on your left. The road soon leaves the village. There is a tall mixed hedge on the right, its shrubs intertwined with ivy and brambles. The fields around here are smaller than in most other parts of Cambridgeshire, with more hedges and trees to break up the scenery.

The road crosses a bridge over a swift stream with yellow flag irises growing in it. Where the road bends left, take the public footpath right (1); this follows a hedge on the right with a field to the left. At the hedge end the path crosses open fields, following telegraph wires. The nature reserve wood is visible beyond fields to the right.

Eventually you reach the edge of a conifer plantation on the right. At the end of this plantation, go right along a farm track. Ahead is Chippenham Fen National Nature Reserve, which you enter through the kissing gate to the right of a five-bar gate. Wooden buildings on the right (2) include a first aid hut and site office, with leaflets about the nature reserve. There is also an information board with a map and, if you're *really* lucky, a warden to chat with.

Keep to the public footpath, which is the main central ride, through the reserve. The ground either side of the path is boggy with reedbeds and alders, and open areas behind the trees. A flowing dyke parallels the path on the left, with aquatic plants growing in it. A few silver birch trees and conifers grow among the alders, and dead trees and log piles abound.

After about half a mile, you come to an interesting open bog (3) fed by the flowing dyke water. This area is mainly reedbeds, but a row of pines grows in front of a ridge ahead to the right.

Go over the stile by the gate. At the end of the path, turn right towards Chippenham. On your left is an old wood behind a wire fence. Take the stile into the next field and continue ahead, following the field edge. Next to the path is a row of pines of all ages (4), from young to dead. The old and dead specimens are drilled with holes, almost certainly the work of woodpeckers.

Leave the nature reserve at the next stile. This track is margined with trees, then hedgerows. Go through the metal gate and turn right along the road towards Chippenham. Just inside the village boundary, go left along Isleham Road, then right at the public footpath sign and

Decaying
log pile.

81

over a stile with a yellow marker arrow. Follow the straight track between horse paddocks. When the main track bends left, go through the fence gap and turn right (5). The path soon emerges into a field. Continue ahead, keeping the hedge on your right. The path reaches some houses and passes between them.

Go left at the road, descending between houses and then fields, to a stream bridge. Just past the bridge, turn right and go over the stile on to the public footpath. Head towards the field corner by a wood, turn right and cross the stream. This stream flows through a field where horses are kept, and follows a belt of trees on the left. The plain square church tower is visible behind trees ahead to the right.

Turn left at the end between gardens, then right at the road, which leads back to the church and lay-by.

History and wildlife

Chippenham Fen has been leased from Chippenham estate and managed by English Nature since the mid 1960s. This 117 hectare National Nature Reserve is a valuable and rare portion of original Cambridgeshire fen. It occupies a shallow peat-filled hollow over chalk bedrock. In places the chalk appears at the surface as grey-white patches among the dark soil.

The clear water of the dykes, ponds and marshes is replenished from springs and rainfall, and excess water drains into the Chippenham River north of the reserve. Other habitats include carr, scrub, mature woodland, chalk meadows and reed beds. Over three hundred wild-flower varieties have been recorded here, including several types of orchid and the very rare Cambridge milk parsley. The reserve is also rich in invertebrates, including more than five hundred species of moths. A few types of invertebrates are only known to exist in this reserve in Britain. Woodpeckers, warblers, woodcock and snipe are among the birds that breed here.

Management of the site involves scrub clearance from the meadows,

Chippenham Fen.

harvesting the hay, cutting the reeds and ensuring that the water level remains high.

In July 2001, a small herd of water buffalo was introduced to graze the meadows and woodland clearings. These animals are ideal for the wet conditions underfoot.

Places of interest

Another nature reserve in the area is Wicken Fen, about six miles west of Chippenham Fen. There is a charge to enter this old and important National Trust site, with its visitor centre and facilities.

Newmarket is famous for its horse racing and breeding, and is home to the National Stud, which runs conducted tours. The National Horseracing Museum has displays about the history of horseracing in England.

East of Chippenham Fen, Burwell Museum has an interesting collection illustrating fen life through the ages, among other things.

APPENDIX I

Societies and Places of Interest

Bedfordshire, Cambridgeshire an Northamptonshire Wildlife Trust, 5 Fulbourn Manor, Fulbourn, Cambridge.
Tel: 01223 880788

Cambridgeshire County Council (Rural Group), Department of Property, Shire Hall, Cambridge, CB3 0AP.
Tel: 01223 317404

Cambridge Preservation Society, Wandlebury Ring, Babraham, Cambridge, CB2 4AE.

Cromwell Museum, Grammar School Walk, Huntingdon.
Tel: 01480 425830

Ely Museum, The Old Gaol, Market Street, Ely.

English Nature, Ham Lane House, Ham Lane, Orton Waterville, Peterborough, PE2 5UR.
Tel: 01733 391100

Ferry Meadows, Nene Park, Peterborough.
Tel: 01733 234443

Fitzwilliam Museum, Trumpington Street, Cambridge, CB2 1RB.
Tel: 01223 332900

Grove House Museum, High Street, Chatteris.

Huntingdonshire District Council (Countryside Project Officer), Planning Department, Pathfinder House, St Mary's Street, Huntingdon, PE18 6TN.
Tel: 01480 388442

Imperial War Museum, Duxford Airfield, Duxford, CB2 4QR.
Tel: 01223 835000

National Horse Racing Museum, 99 High Street, Newmarket, CB8 8JL. *Tel:* 01638 667333

National Stud, Newmarket, CB8 0XE.
Tel: 01638 666789

Nene Valley Steam Railway, Wansford Station, Wansford, near Peterborough. Open weekends mid Feb to end Oct.
Tel: 01780 784444

Oliver Cromwell's House, 29 St Mary's Street, Ely.
Tel: 01353 662062

Peakirk Waterfowl gardens, Peakirk, near Peterborough.
Tel: 01733 252271.

Ramsey Rural Museum, Ramsey.
Tel: 01487 813949

Royal Society for the Protection of Birds, The Lodge, Sandy, Bedfordshire, SG19 2DL.
Tel: 01767 680551

APPENDIX II

Tourist Information Centres

Cambridge – Wheeler Street, Cambridge.
Tel: 01223 322640

Ely – Oliver Cromwell's House, 29 St Mary's Street, Ely CB7 4HF.
Tel: 01353 662062

Huntingdon – Princes Street, Huntingdon, PE29 3PH.
Tel: 01480 388591

St Neots – The Old Court, 8 New Street, St Neots, PE19 1AE.
Tel: 01480 388788

LOCAL TITLES
PUBLISHED BY JOHN NICKALLS
PUBLICATIONS

A GARLAND OF WAVENEY VALLEY
TALES
A compilation of illustrated tales from
Suffolk of yesteryear.

A LEVEL COUNTRY
Sketches of its Fenland folk and history.

A PHARMACIST'S TALE
The joys, delights and disappointments
encountered preserving pharmacy history.

CURIOSITIES OF NORFOLK
A county guide to the unusual.

GREAT OUSE COUNTRY
Sketches of its riverside folk and history
from source to mouth.

MELTON CONSTABLE, BRISTON &
DISTRICT – BOOK ONE
A portrait in old picture postcards.

MELTON CONSTABLE, BRISTON &
DISTRICT – BOOK TWO
A further portrait in old picture postcards.

NATURE TRAILS IN
NORTHAMPTONSHIRE
A series of illustrated walks.

NEWMARKET, TOWN AND TURF
A pictorial tour.

NORTH NORFOLK
A portrait in old picture postcards.

NORWICH – THEN AND NOW
A look at the city through old postcards
and modern photographs.

IN AND AROUND NORWICH – THEN
AND NOW
A further look at Norwich and district.

NORWICH – THEN AND NOW
A third selection of old picture postcards.

ROBBER BARONS AND FIGHTING
BISHOPS
The Norman influence in East Anglia.

SHIRES, SALES AND PIGS
The story of an Ely family of
Auctioneers. George Comins,
1856–1997.

SUFFOLK'S LIFEBOATS
A portrait in postcards and photographs.

S'WONDERFUL
A symphony of musical memories.

'SMARVELLOUS
More musical memories.

TIPPLE & TEASHOP RAMBLES
IN NORTHAMPTONSHIRE
A series of illustrated walks.